THE MICK JAGGER STORY

The Man Who Changed Rock Music

Lee L. Mull

TABLE OF CONTENTS

INTRODUCTION

In the annals of rock 'n' roll history, few names carry the weight and resonance of Sir Michael Philip Jagger. With an illustrious career spanning over six decades, Mick Jagger has etched his name into the fabric of music history, leaving an indelible mark as one of the most influential and celebrated figures in popular music.

Born on July 26, 1943, in Dartford, England, Jagger's journey to stardom was extraordinary. From his early days at the London School of Economics to his pivotal decision to embrace the call of music, the path ahead was destined to change the face of rock forever.

Together with guitarist Keith Richards, Jagger co-founded the Rolling Stones in the early 1960s, and little did they know that their partnership would give birth to a musical legacy that defied time and captivated generations of fans worldwide. Their songwriting prowess remains unparalleled, solidifying them as one of history's most successful duos. Jagger's unmistakable voice and his captivating stage presence became the band's trademark.

The Rolling Stone's live performances, fueled by the incomparable guitar style of Richards, became the stuff of legends, commanding an unwavering following that endured through the ages.

But the life of Mick Jagger was not confined to the spotlight alone. Beyond the electrifying performances and chart-topping hits, he was no stranger to controversy, finding himself in the headlines for his romantic involvements and run-ins with the law. His persona as a countercultural figure cemented his status as not just a musician but also a symbol of rebellion and artistic expression.

Venturing into acting, Jagger showcased his versatility in films such as "Performance" and "Ned Kelly," demonstrating an artistic depth beyond the stage. As the years progressed, his solo career and various side projects showcased his creative ambition, pushing the boundaries of his artistry even further. Jagger's journey has been intertwined with various relationships and personal connections throughout his life. From his marriage to Bianca Pérez-Mora Macias to his experiences as a father of eight, his private life has mirrored the intensity and complexity of his musical endeavors.

The accolades bestowed upon Mick Jagger are countless, with numerous inductions into prestigious music halls of fame and recognition for his unparalleled achievements in the charts. Knighted for his services to popular music, Jagger's impact extended even to the world of paleontology, with prehistoric creatures being named in his honor.

As we embark on this biography, we invite you to delve deep into the life, career, and enigmatic persona of Mick Jagger. This captivating exploration will chronicle the highs and lows, the triumphs and challenges, and the unwavering passion that has defined the journey of a true rock 'n' roll legend.

From his humble beginnings in Dartford to the global stage, from intimate romances to rebellious anthems, the story of Mick Jagger is a tapestry of music, fame, and human complexity. Join us on this unparalleled voyage into the heart of a living legend as we unveil the essence of Mick Jagger - a man who has forever etched his name in the annals of music history.

CHAPTER I

Early Life

Mick Jagger, a name now synonymous with rock 'n' roll royalty, was born on a summer's day, July 26, 1943, into a middle-class family in the charming town of Dartford, Kent. His father, Basil Fanshawe "Joe" Jagger, was more than just a gymnast and physical education teacher; he was a pioneer who played a vital role in popularizing basketball across Britain. The apple didn't fall far from the tree regarding athleticism, as Mick's paternal grandfather, David Ernest Jagger, was also an esteemed teacher.

On the other hand, Mick's mother, Eva Ensley Mary (née Scutts), brought a touch of English heritage from her birthplace in Sydney, Australia. A talented hairdresser, she was politically active within the Conservative Party in the United Kingdom. In 1940, Joe and Eva tied the knot at the Holy Trinity Church in Dartford, laying the foundation for the Jagger family's journey.

Mick Jagger's childhood was enriched by the presence of a younger brother named Chris, born on December 19, 1947.

As fate would have it, both siblings would eventually find themselves entangled in the world of music, creating a harmonious bond through their shared passion.

While it seemed that Mick might follow in his father's footsteps into physical education, destiny had different plans for him. Even as a child, Mick's unmistakable gift for singing set him apart.

During his early schooling years at Wentworth Primary School in Dartford, fate paved the way for Mick's musical destiny. September 1950 marked the momentous meeting between Mick Jagger and a future musical comrade, Keith Richards. Both classmates discovered a shared passion for music that would one day change the course of history.

After the Jagger family's move to Wilmington, Kent, in 1954, Mick's life continued to evolve. Passing the eleven-plus examination, he embarked on a new chapter at Dartford Grammar School, where the foundations of his artistic journey were further nurtured. Dartford Grammar School would later be celebrated as the venue for the Mick Jagger Centre, a tribute to the enduring impact of this musical prodigy.

However, Mick Jagger and Keith Richards lost touch when they attended separate schools, as life often spins complex narratives. However, the universe had more for young musicians than they imagined. The mid-1950s saw Mick's music career take flight as he teamed up with his close friend Dick Taylor to form a garage band. They fervently played the tunes of blues legends like Muddy Waters, Chuck Berry, Little Richard, Howlin' Wolf, and Bo Diddley, sowing the seeds of their future musical odyssey.

Fate's whimsical dance brought Mick Jagger and Keith Richards back together. On a memorable day, October 17, 1961, they encountered each other once more on Platform Two of Dartford railway station. Mick's collection of Chuck Berry and Muddy Waters records caught Keith's attention, revealing an electrifying shared interest in rhythm and blues. Their cosmic connection manifested into a musical partnership that would soon turn the world of music on its head. Little did anyone know that the chance reunion at Dartford station was just the prologue to a much grander story.

As their shared passion ignited, Mick, Keith, and Dick Taylor began meeting regularly, laying the foundation for a musical adventure that would shake the music industry's core. Soon, they would be joined by Brian Jones, a gifted guitarist, and the Blues Boys were born, heralding the rise of a legendary group that would become a household name—the Rolling Stones.

With dreams of musical stardom taking root, Mick Jagger left school in 1961, having completed seven O-levels and two A-levels. He set up residence with Keith Richards in a flat at Edith Grove in Chelsea, London, where they would share their love for music, forming a profound friendship that would withstand the test of time.

While Mick and Keith embarked on their musical journey, Mick did not shy away from pursuing knowledge. As an undergraduate student at the London School of Economics, he focused on finance and accounting, even entertaining thoughts of becoming a journalist or a politician—careers that he whimsically compared to that of a pop star.

The stage was set for the birth of a musical revolution. As the 1960s rolled in, Brian Jones, Mick Jagger, and Keith Richards collaborated with a music ensemble, Blues Incorporated, led by the revered Alexis Korner.

It was a lucky moment in history, for it was here that the sparks of the Rolling Stones would ignite. Mick's mesmerizing voice took center stage, and the young men embarked on a creative journey that would redefine the very essence of rock 'n' roll.

Chapter 1 begins a legendary tale of unparalleled talent, unbridled ambition, and the triumph of dreams over adversity in this intricate tapestry of music and destiny. The young boy from Dartford would become one of the most influential figures in music history—Mick Jagger, the enigmatic soul behind the Rolling Stones' resounding success.

CHAPTER 2

Career

In the early 1960s, a group of ambitious young musicians gathered in the dimly lit basement of a club near London's Ealing Broadway tube station. Little did they know that this humble beginning would mark the genesis of one of the most legendary rock bands in history - The Rolling Stones. Led by the magnetic force of their frontman, Mick Jagger, the band's journey from obscurity to global superstardom is a tale of passion, creativity, and unrelenting determination.

As the band's name evolved from the Rollin' Stones, inspired by one of their favorite Muddy Waters songs, to the more formal "Rolling Stones," their lineup solidified with Mick Jagger as the enigmatic frontman, Keith Richards as the iconic guitarist, Brian Jones, Ian Stewart, Dick Taylor, and Tony Chapman. However, history plays tricks, as Richards would later reveal that the drummer on their first appearance was Mick Avory, not Tony Chapman, challenging the established narrative.

During a transformative five-month residency at Eel Pie Island Hotel, the band honed their skills and crafted their unique sound, laying the foundation for a career-shaping music history. As they delved into the world of American rhythm and blues, covering the likes of Chuck Berry and Bo Diddley, The Rolling Stones found early success with cover versions like "It's All Over Now" and "Little Red Rooster," earning them their first UK No. 1 hits.

But the duo of Jagger and Richards sparked a creative revolution within the band. Encouraged by manager Andrew Loog Oldham, they began writing their songs, with "As Tears Go By" becoming one of their early collaborations, crafted for the young singer Marianne Faithfull. However, with "(I Can't Get No) Satisfaction," they catapulted into international stardom, becoming rebellious symbols of rock 'n' roll. Behind the scenes, The Rolling Stones faced challenges, including legal battles, drug controversies, and personal conflicts. Amidst it all, they continued to produce groundbreaking albums, like "Beggars Banquet," "Let It Bleed," and "Sticky Fingers," which solidified their place in rock history.

Tragedy struck with the untimely death of Brian Jones in 1969, just before the iconic Hyde Park concert dedicated to him. The band pressed on, welcoming Mick Taylor as their new guitarist and releasing more hits like "Brown Sugar" and "Angie."

The 1970s brought new experiments in music and style, with Jagger leading the way. He ventured into solo projects while maintaining a central role in The Rolling Stones. Their 1981 album "Tattoo You" proved to be a massive success, but behind the scenes, tensions between Jagger and Richards reached an all-time high, threatening to unravel the band.

Yet, like true rock 'n' roll survivors, The Rolling Stones persevered. They continued to produce hits, tour the world, and break records. Jagger's solo career flourished during this time, showcasing his versatility and artistry beyond the band's confines.

Through the decades, The Rolling Stones remained a living testament to the power of rock 'n' roll. Their charisma, passion, and magnetic energy kept them relevant to audiences worldwide.

They weathered storms, celebrated triumphs, and etched their names into the very fabric of music history.

As we journey through the history of The Rolling Stones, we'll witness the raw human stories behind the glitz and glamour of stardom. We'll explore the moments of vulnerability, the artistic highs, and the enduring spirit that have made them one of the most iconic bands in the world.

CHAPTER 3

Personal Life

Mick Jagger is a true rock 'n' roll icon. He is the frontman of The Rolling Stones, one of history's most successful and influential bands. But Jagger is more than just a musician; he is also a complex and contradictory figure who has lived a life of love, music, and philanthropy.

Born into a world of music and raised in the vibrant era of the swinging '60s, Jagger's journey through fame and relationships reads like a riveting tale of highs and lows. As we explore the chapters of his life, we encounter the women who have played significant roles in his heart and the children who have enriched his legacy.

In the early days, Jagger's heart belonged to Chrissie Shrimpton, with whom he shared a love story from 1963 to 1966. They were one of the most glamorous couples of the era, and their relationship was often splashed across the tabloids. He was entwined with Marianne Faithfull, an English singer-songwriter and actress.

They created unforgettable music together, including the hauntingly poignant "Sister Morphine." As the years unfolded, Jagger's magnetic charisma led him to American singer Marsha Hunt. Although she was married, they embarked on a relationship. This union resulted in the birth of his first child, Karis Hunt Jagger, a symbol of love and complexity. Meanwhile, the infamous "Brown Sugar," a song from The Rolling Stones' album "Sticky Fingers," was inspired by the alluring Hunt.

In 1971, Jagger walked down the aisle with Bianca Pérez-Mora Macias in a lavish Catholic ceremony in Saint-Tropez, France. Their union brought forth a daughter, Jade Sheena Jezebel Jagger. But even amid the glamour, the marriage faced its trials, leading to their separation in 1977.

It was in the late '70s when Jagger's path crossed with American model Jerry Hall, and they embarked on a journey of love and family. An unofficial private marriage ceremony in Bali in 1990 sealed their bond, and the couple welcomed four children: Elizabeth 'Lizzie' Scarlett, James Leroy Augustin, Georgia May Ayeesha, and Gabriel Luke Beauregard Jagger.

While love and family seemed to thrive, Jagger's life was not without its share of romantic entanglements. An affair with Italian singer/model Carla Bruni from 1991 to 1994 brought further complexity, as did a liaison with Brazilian model Luciana Gimenez, which resulted in the birth of his seventh child, Lucas Maurice Morad Jagger.

Despite an unofficial marriage, Jagger's relationship with Hall faced legal challenges when it was declared invalid by the High Court of England and Wales in 1999. Later, a romance with English model Sophie Dahl captured headlines in the early 2000s.

As time went on, Jagger found solace and love in the arms of fashion designer L'Wren Scott. Their relationship blossomed from 2001 until her tragic suicide in 2014, impacting Jagger's life. He set up the L'Wren Scott scholarship at London's Central Saint Martins College to honor her memory.

From the depths of loss, Jagger found love again with American ballet dancer Melanie Hamrick. Despite the age gap, their connection transcended boundaries, and in 2016, they welcomed their son, Deveraux Octavian Basil Jagger.

Beyond the glitz and glamour, Jagger's heart beats for philanthropy. An advocate for music in schools, he patronizes The Mick Jagger Centre in Dartford and sponsors local schools' music programs through the Red Rooster Programme.

A devoted cricket fan and avid England national football team follower, Jagger's interests extend beyond music and fame. With an estimated net worth of US$500 million, he remains one of music's most recognizable figures, leaving an indelible mark on the world.

The life of Mick Jagger is a tale of love, music, and philanthropy - a unique journey that has touched hearts, influenced generations, and shaped the landscape of rock 'n' roll history. As we delve deeper into the chapters of his life, we witness a man whose legacy reaches far beyond the stage, leaving a lasting impression on both the world of entertainment and the hearts of those he's touched along the way. Jagger's life is a testament to the power of love, music, and the human spirit. He has shown us that it is possible to achieve great things, even in the face of adversity.

He has inspired us to follow our dreams, to never give up on love, and to make a difference in the world.

CHAPTER 4

Controversy

As with any larger-than-life figure, controversy has never been far from Mick Jagger's doorstep. From his provocative stage presence to his stormy personal life, the enigmatic frontman of The Rolling Stones has found himself at the epicenter of countless debates and scandals throughout his illustrious career. The 1960s was a decade of rebellion and revolution, and Jagger embodied the spirit of the times with unapologetic enthusiasm.

As The Rolling Stones gained notoriety for their rebellious attitude and explicit lyrics, they faced opposition from conservative circles and government authorities. Their infamous 1967 song "Let's Spend the Night Together" sparked outrage and censorship, challenging societal norms and pushing the boundaries of acceptability. The tragic events at the Altamont Free Concert in 1969 remain haunting in The Rolling Stones' history. The ill-fated festival organized as a West Coast counterpart to Woodstock, turned into a nightmarish scene of violence and chaos.

The fatal stabbing of a concertgoer by a Hells Angels member, who was providing security, cast a shadow over the band and raised questions about the perils of counterculture and rock's influence on society. Jagger's onstage persona exuded raw sexuality and androgynous charm, pushing the boundaries of gender norms. His flamboyant stage outfits and provocative performances challenged traditional notions of masculinity, earning both adoration from fans and criticism from conservative quarters.

In a time when discussions of sexuality were still taboo, Jagger's audacity added fuel to the fires of controversy. The rock 'n' roll lifestyle of excess and hedonism took its toll on Jagger, leading to several brushes with the law. In 1967, he was arrested for drug possession, and in 1970, he faced a lengthy legal battle over a drug-related arrest in England. Despite these legal woes, Jagger's resilience and popularity remained undeterred, further fueling the ongoing debates surrounding the relationship between rock stars and drug culture. The pages of Jagger's personal life have been rife with drama and turbulence. His high-profile relationships, numerous affairs, and unconventional choices have been a constant source of media scrutiny.

Jagger's love life has been a rollercoaster of passion and controversy, from the dissolution of his marriage to Bianca Pérez-Mora Macias to his tumultuous liaisons with model Jerry Hall and Italian singer/model Carla Bruni. As the years have passed, Jagger has defied age, continuing to rock stages worldwide with relentless energy.

While admirers applaud his enduring spirit and vitality, critics raise questions about the appropriateness of a septuagenarian performing with the same enthusiasm as in his younger days. Yet, Jagger remains unyielding, proving that age is merely a number in rock 'n' roll. Despite the controversies surrounding him, Jagger's influence on music, culture, and fashion is undeniable. He has catalyzed change, pushing societal boundaries and challenging norms. His charisma, stage presence, and artistry have inspired countless artists and performers, leaving an indelible mark on the entertainment world.

In this chapter, we have explored the many faces of Mick Jagger - the rock icon who has courted controversy throughout his storied career. From defying societal norms to facing legal challenges, his life has been a whirlwind of tumultuous events and daring choices.

Despite the controversies that have swirled around him, one thing remains clear: Mick Jagger's impact on the world of music and culture is immeasurable, and his influence will continue reverberating through the ages.

CHAPTER 5

Acting Career

Mick Jagger, an iconic figure in rock music, has also proven himself a talented actor. His journey into acting began in the late 1960s with the cult classic film Performance, where he portrayed a bisexual rock star in a drug-fueled love triangle. The film's success established him as a legitimate actor.

Throughout the 1970s, Jagger took on various roles in films like Ned Kelly and Savages, showcasing his willingness to explore diverse characters. Although only some of these ventures achieved the same level of success as Performance, they highlighted his passion for acting.

In the 1980s, Jagger focused more on his music career, but he still appeared in films like Freejack and Running Out of Luck, displaying his commitment to both crafts.

The 1990s marked a triumphant return for Jagger with the film Bent, where he portrayed a gay man imprisoned in a Nazi concentration camp. His powerful performance earned him a Golden Globe nomination, reinforcing his versatility as an actor.

In the 21st century, Jagger continued to act, starring in films such as The Man from Elysian Fields and Shine a Light, maintaining his magnetic presence on the big screen.

Described as charismatic and magnetic, Jagger's acting style effortlessly commands the screen. He convincingly portrays a wide range of characters, from rock stars to gangsters to concentration camp survivors, captivating audiences with his performances.

Throughout his career, Jagger's passion for creative expression has remained undiminished, making him a respected figure in both the music and acting worlds. His work continues to entertain and inspire audiences worldwide.

CHAPTER 6

Awards and Honours

In the vast annals of rock 'n' roll history, one name emerges as a living legend, an embodiment of unbridled energy, and an enduring symbol of raw, untamed charisma: Mick Jagger. As the magnetic frontman of The Rolling Stones, Jagger's electrifying presence has transcended generations, leaving an indelible mark on the music industry and popular culture.

From the iconic stage moves that captivated audiences to the unmistakable voice that resonated with millions, Mick Jagger's journey from a young, ambitious dreamer to a global superstar is a tale of triumph, turbulence, and unwavering passion. Venturing deep into the fascinating life of Mick Jagger, this biography unravels the highs and lows of a career that has spanned decades.

From the smoky clubs of London's swinging '60s, where The Rolling Stones first ignited their fiery ascent, to the sold-out stadiums that pulsated with the rhythm of rock 'n' roll across the globe, every chapter of Jagger's life unfolds as a captivating rollercoaster ride.

Yet, it is not only the stage that bore witness to Mick Jagger's greatness; his impact resonates far beyond the realms of music. Throughout his illustrious journey, he has been bestowed with prestigious accolades and enduring tributes, affirming his profound imprint on the world. In 2002, a momentous honor was bestowed upon him, transcending mere fame and acclaim.

As part of the Queen's Birthday Honors, Mick Jagger was knighted for his exceptional services to popular music. A defining moment in his life, the revered accolade was presented to him in December 2003 by none other than The Prince of Wales. The ceremony, graced by his father and beloved daughters, Karis and Elizabeth, bore witness to a deeply emotional occasion. While Jagger admitted that the knighthood did not hold overwhelming personal significance, he was touched by the immense pride it instilled in his father.

The bond between father and son grew more vigorous, infused with a shared sense of honor and dignity. Notably, Mick Jagger's profound impact on the music world was eternally immortalized in the hallowed halls of the American Rock and Roll Hall of Fame.

In 1989, alongside his indomitable Rolling Stones bandmates, Jagger received this prestigious induction, celebrating their remarkable musical journey and the timeless influence they wielded over the genre. The solemn ceremony also paid tribute to the late Brian Jones and Ian Stewart, accentuating the band's enduring legacy and the profound mark they left on the history of rock music.

Beyond American shores, The Rolling Stones' influence was no less potent. The year 2004 bore witness to a momentous event as they were among the esteemed inaugural inductees into the UK Music Hall of Fame. This distinguished recognition was reserved for the most iconic and influential contributors to British music history, solidifying the band's place as global musical titans.

But Mick Jagger's captivating legacy reached even further into paleontology, where his name became intertwined with the mysteries of ancient history. In 2014, the world was introduced to two ancient species that bore the iconic rock star's name, forever connecting him to the wonders of prehistoric life. The Jaggermeryx naida, affectionately known as "Jagger's water nymph," emerged as a 19-million-year-old species of 'long-legged pig,' discovered through fossil jaw fragments found in Egypt. The trilobite species Aegrotocatellus jaggeri, lovingly dubbed the "Jagger trilobite," added another chapter to the enduring fascination with Mick Jagger's impact on multiple fields.

As if ancient pigs and trilobites weren't enough, a whimsical and witty tribute from the scientific community marked Mick Jagger's 75th birthday. Seven fossil stoneflies were named after present and former members of The Rolling Stones, celebrating the band's legacy in entomology. Petroperla mickjaggeri and Lapisperla keithrichardsi, two of the named species, found their place within the newly created family Petroperlidae, aptly named to honor the band's iconic moniker. These captivating creatures affectionately became known as the "Rolling Stoneflies," a lighthearted tribute to the timeless influence of The Rolling Stones.

The journey of Mick Jagger remains an awe-inspiring tale of brilliance and creativity that extends far beyond the stage. As the spotlight of accolades and tributes continues to shine on him, Jagger's impact on multiple fields, from music to the sciences, reaffirms his status as an enduring cultural icon. In the following chapters, we will delve deeper into Mick's personal life, his collaborations, and the musical milestones that have defined his extraordinary career, celebrating the enigmatic essence of an icon of rock 'n' roll who ranks among the best ever.

CHAPTER 7

Legacy

Mick Jagger's magnetic presence on stage and impact on the world of music has been revolutionary. British dramatist and novelist Philip Norman succinctly captured the essence of Jagger's influence when he remarked that Jagger's power over 'young people' was not fundamentally harmless, unlike anything witnessed before. Elvis Presley, the King of Rock 'n' Roll himself, paled in comparison to the wholly and disturbingly physical effect that Jagger had on his audience. Jagger's early performances with The Rolling Stones in the 1960s were akin to witnessing a male ballet dancer, with his conflicting and colliding sexuality leaving a lasting impression on those who experienced his electric presence.

Academics and musicologists have extensively analyzed Jagger's performance style, focusing on its impact on gender, image, and sexuality. Sheila Whiteley, a renowned musicologist, noted that Jagger's stage persona broke traditional definitions of gendered masculinity, laying the foundation for self-invention and sexual fluidity that is now integral to contemporary youth culture.

Jagger's performances also contributed significantly to the British tradition of popular music, where singing became a form of acting, leaving audiences questioning the relationship between the singer and his own words.

Jagger's voice, described as a powerful expressive tool, transcends the mere delivery of lyrics; it becomes a conduit for communicating emotions and expressing an alternative vision of society. To evoke "virility and unrestrained passion," he adopted techniques inspired by African American preachers and gospel singers, incorporating roars, guttural belts, and nasal and raspy sounds. In recognition of Jagger's groundbreaking vocal style, Steven Van Zandt acknowledged that his acceptance on pop radio was a turning point in rock & roll, opening doors for future artists to explore their unique voices.

Over time, Mick Jagger has evolved into the quintessential rock frontman, paving the way for modern music industry pioneers. The Telegraph aptly hails him as "the Rolling Stone who changed music," a sentiment that numerous music enthusiasts and critics echoed. His influence extends far beyond the stage, with contemporary British rock musicians incorporating elements of his onstage presence into their personas. In its accolade, Billboard ranks him among the best rock leads of all time, emphasizing how his swagger and style brought unparalleled sexiness to rock music, igniting a legacy that continues to inspire to this day.

Jagger's profound influence has also been recognized by fellow musicians, such as David Bowie, who once dreamt of emulating his idol's magnetic stage presence. His status as a sex symbol has transcended time, morphing into a mother figure for many admirers. Fellow artists, including Lenny Kravitz, consider Jagger's vocals sophisticated and stunning, embodying a perfection that leaves a lasting impact.

As a mentor and advisor, Jagger has also played a significant role in the careers of aspiring musicians, seeking out newcomers to the music industry and offering his guidance. Beyond his musical talents, Jagger's business understanding and ability to surround himself with capable executives have been recognized as integral to the success of The Rolling Stones and their enduring impact on the music industry.

Remarkably, as Jagger has aged, his vitality and energy continue to captivate audiences, prompting awe and admiration from his peers. He embodies what some authors describe as a "Dionysian archetype" of "eternal youth," a symbol of timeless rebellion synonymous with rock culture and its pursuit of eternal energy and passion.

Despite his remarkable life and career, Jagger has resisted the temptation to write an autobiography, preferring to let his performances and music speak for themselves. Nevertheless, numerous unauthorized biographies have attempted to delve into the enigmatic persona of Mick Jagger, a testament to his enduring allure and lasting influence.

Watts, The Rolling Stones drummer, aptly summed up Jagger's character, describing him as the least egotistical person who always puts the band's interests above all else. Jagger's humility and willingness to evolve as an artist are a testament to his enduring impact, and he remains an eternal symbol of rock 'n' roll's unyielding spirit. As we delve deeper into the intricacies of Mick Jagger's life and career, we will discover the man behind the legend, the visionary behind the performer, and the essence of Mick Jagger, the musical maverick who continues to shape the landscape of rock music and popular culture.

CONCLUSION

The captivating journey through the life and legacy of Mick Jagger reveals an unparalleled force in the world of music and a true cultural icon. From his electrifying stage presence to his groundbreaking vocal style, Jagger has left an indelible mark on the history of rock 'n' roll. His ability to embody conflicting and colliding expressions of sexuality while breaking traditional gender norms has inspired a generation of musicians and shaped contemporary youth culture.

As the charismatic frontman of The Rolling Stones, Mick Jagger's influence extends far beyond the realm of music. He has been hailed as one of the most influential and beloved leads in rock history, and his impact on the music industry is immeasurable. From receiving a knighthood for his services to popular music to being inducted into the Rock and Roll Hall of Fame, Jagger's contributions have been widely recognized and celebrated.

Beyond accolades and honors, Jagger's continued vitality and ability to captivate audiences even as he ages serve as a testament to his enduring passion for his craft.

He embodies the eternal spirit of rock 'n' roll, a Dionysian archetype of perpetual youth, forever pushing the boundaries of creative expression and breaking barriers in his unique way. As a mentor and role model, Jagger has guided aspiring musicians and continues to leave a lasting impact on the music industry's next generation. His influence transcends generations, with contemporary artists acknowledging his profound effect on their musical journeys.

Despite the temptation of writing an autobiography, Jagger's decision to let his performances and music speak for themselves only adds to the mystique of this enigmatic musical legend. He remains a symbol of humility, always putting the interests of his band and music ahead of personal acclaim.

Mick Jagger's journey from a young dreamer in the swinging '60s to an enduring rock legend has been extraordinary. His relentless pursuit of creativity, authenticity, and reinvention continues to inspire millions around the world. The story of Mick Jagger is not just one of fame and success but also passion, dedication, and a relentless pursuit of artistic excellence.

As we bid farewell to this heartwarming exploration of Mick Jagger's life, we are reminded of the power of music to transcend time and generations, leaving an everlasting impact on the human soul. Mick Jagger's legacy will forever resonate, and his contributions to the world of music and culture will continue to shape history for years.

Made in the USA
Columbia, SC
15 December 2023

28689914R00024